Published by Creative Education
P.O. Box 227, Mankato, Minnesota 56002
Creative Education is an imprint of
The Creative Company
www.thecreativecompany.us

Design and production by The Design Lab
Art direction by Rita Marshall
Printed by Corporate Graphics in the
United States of America

Photographs by Alamy (Steve Bloom Images),
Dreamstime (Eric Gevaert, Darren Green, Hilton
Kotze), Getty Images (Theo Allofs, John Dominis),
iStockphoto (Ewan Chesser, Eric Isselée, Peter
Malsbury, Tatiana Morozova, Graeme Purdy,
Kristian Sekulic, Peter Ten Broecke)

Library of Congress Cataloging-in-Publication Data
Riggs, Kate.
Leopards / by Kate Riggs.
p. cm. — (Amazing animals)
Summary: A basic exploration of the appearance,
behavior, and habitat of leopards, Earth's fourth-
largest cats. Also included is a story from folklore
explaining why leopards and baboons don't
get along.
Includes bibliographical references and index.
ISBN 978-1-60818-110-0
1. Leopard—Juvenile literature. I. Title. II. Series.
QL737.C23R5384 2012
599.75'54—dc22   2010049130

CPSIA: 031412 PO1557

9 8 7 6 5 4 3 2

LIVING ANIMALS

LEOPARDS

BY KATE RIGGS

CREATIVE EDUCATION

Leopards are the fourth-biggest cats in the world

Leopards are big cats.
There are nine kinds of leopard. Most live on the **continents** of Africa and Asia. One kind lives in the country of Saudi Arabia.

continents Earth's seven big pieces of land

Leopards have bodies covered with spotted fur. Their fur looks like a cheetah's fur. But leopards' spots are different from cheetahs' spots. Leopards' spots are black with brown or golden centers.

The spots on a leopard's face are usually solid black

A male leopard weighs up to 200 pounds (91 kg). Females weigh about 120 pounds (54 kg). A leopard grows to be six feet (1.8 m) long. Its tail is two to three feet (60–90 cm) long.

Leopards can run as fast as 36 miles (58 km) per hour

Most leopards live in forests and grasslands. A leopard's spotted and golden-colored fur helps it hide in the rocks and tall grasses. Some leopards live in drier lands called deserts. Leopards in these places have fur that is a lighter yellow. This helps them blend in with sand.

A leopard can easily hide when it wants to

Leopards like to carry food into trees

Leopards eat meat. Some of their favorite **prey** to catch and eat are baboons (*bah-BOONZ*) and gazelles (*gah-ZELZ*). Sometimes leopards eat monkeys and **rodents**, too.

prey animals that are killed and eaten by other animals

rodents animals, like rats and mice, that have sharp front teeth, hair or fur, and feed their babies with milk

Cubs are born blind and weigh about one pound (454 g)

A mother leopard has two or three **cubs** at a time. At first, the mother moves her cubs from place to place. She does this to keep them safe from other **predators**. Hyenas, lions, and crocodiles sometimes kill leopard cubs. When the cubs are four months old, they learn how to hunt. Wild leopards can live up to 15 years.

cubs baby leopards

predators animals that kill and eat other animals

Most leopards live alone. They stay in an area called a home range. A leopard guards its home range to make sure other leopards do not try to live there.

Leopards use trees in their home range to store food

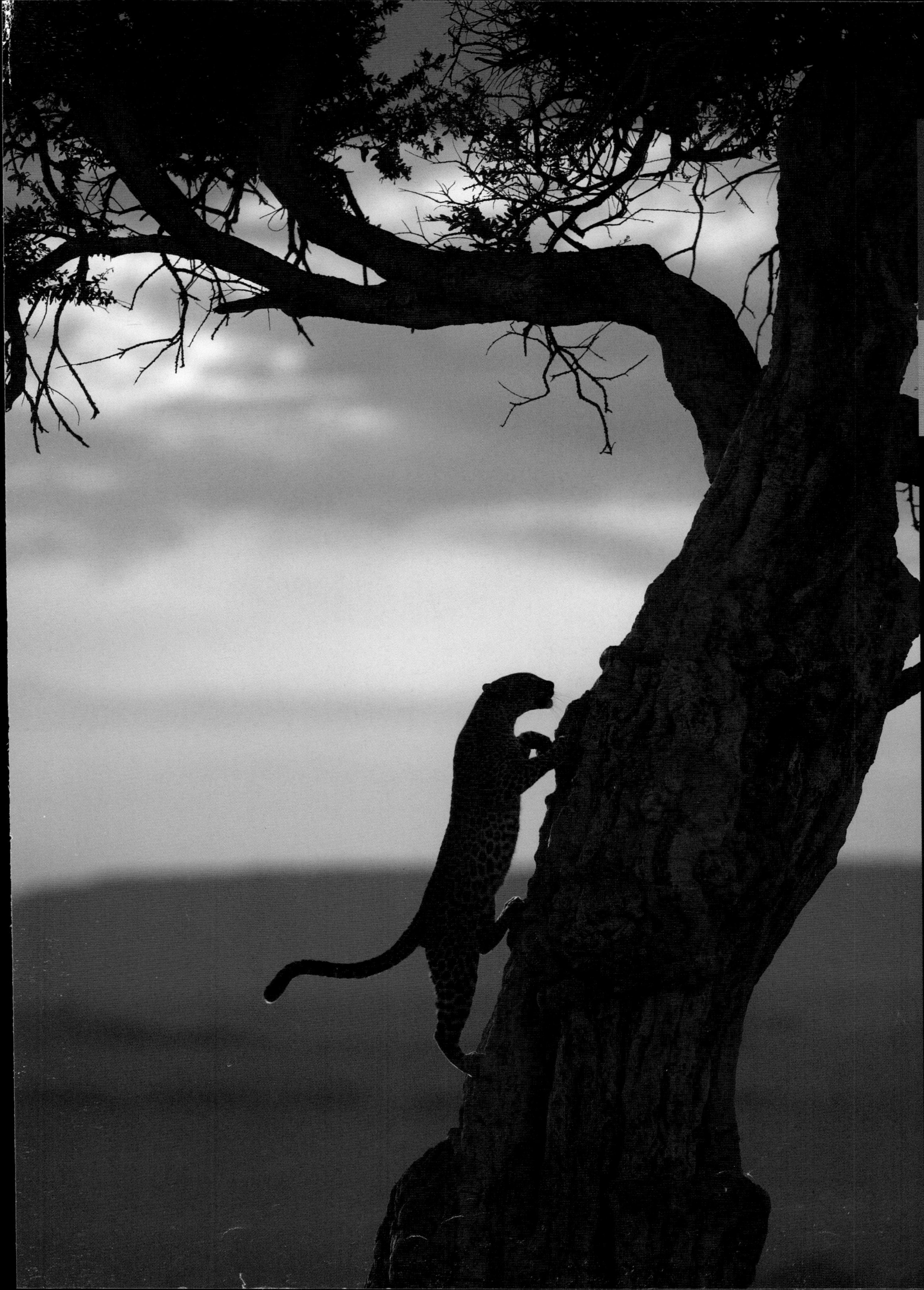

Leopards hunt in the morning or at night. They do not like to hunt when it is very hot. Leopards sneak up on their prey and then pounce. Leopards sleep for about 12 hours a day.

Even at rest, a leopard is ready to spring into action

Today, some people go to Africa or Asia to see leopards in the wild. Other people visit zoos to see leopards. It is exciting to see these big, spotted cats up-close!

A leopard may roar to scare animals or people away

A *Leopard Story*

Why do leopards and baboons not get along? People in South Africa used to tell a story about this. Long ago, leopards and baboons were friends. But one day, when Baboon was helping Leopard catch an animal for lunch, Baboon fell asleep. Leopard was very angry and wanted to eat Baboon instead. Baboon got away by swinging into the trees. Leopards and baboons were never friends again.

Read More

Huggins-Cooper, Lynn. *Big Cats*. North Mankato, Minn.: Smart Apple Media, 2007.

Walker, Sarah. *Eye Wonder: Big Cats*. New York: DK Publishing, 2002.

Web Sites

National Geographic Coloring Book: Leopard Pages
http://www.nationalgeographic.com/coloringbook/leopards.html
This site has a picture of a leopard to print out and color.

San Diego Zoo's Animal Bytes: Leopard
http://www.sandiegozoo.org/animalbytes/t-leopard.html
This site has leopard facts and photos.

Index